THE
MILLER AND HIS MEN.

A Melo=Drama,

IN TWO ACTS.

BY
ISAACK POCOCK,

AUTHOR OF

" The Robber's Wife," " John of Paris," " Hit or Miss,"
" Magpie and the Maid," &c.

THE MUSIC BY
SIR HENRY BISHOP.

THOMAS HAILES LACY,

89, STRAND,

(Opposite Southampton Street, Covent Garden Market,)

LONDON.

As performed at the Theatre Royal Haymarket, (under the management of Mr. Buckstone),
on Monday, April 22nd, 1861.

THE MILLER AND HIS MEN.

The new Scenery and Effects by

MR. FREDERICK FENTON.

The Dresses by Mr. BARNETT and Miss CHERRY.   The Properties by Mr. FOSTER.   The Machinery by Mr. OLIVER WALES.

The original Music by the late

SIR HENRY BISHOP.

The Music conducted by Mr. D. SPILLANE, who has also adapted an additional Chorus and Bohemian Dance at the
end of the First Act.

GRINDOFF (the Miller) ...	...	Mr. HOWE.
LOTHAIR (a young Peasant)	...	Mr. W. FARREN.
COUNT FRIBERG ...	...	Mr. E. VILLIERS.
KARL (his Servant) ...	...	Mr. COMPTON.
KELMAR (an old Cottager) ...	...	Mr. ROGERS.
GOLOTZ } (Lieutenants of the Band)	...	{ Mr. WORRELL.
RIBER }		Mr. CHARLES LECLERCQ.
*ZINGARA CHIEF ...	...	Mr. COURTNEY.
*HIS SON ...	...	Mr. ARTHUR LECLERCQ.

The full and efficient Chorus by Millers—Mr. Weathersby, Mr. James, and Messrs. Miller, Woollidge, Evelyn, Grieves,
Cheese, Whitehouse, Fitzgihton, Banks, Ball, Coleman, Cowlrick, Sherwood, Hyne, Gould, and Hopgood.

KREUTZ ...	...	Master ALEXANDER.
CLAUDINE (Daughter of Kelmar) ...	...	Miss FLORENCE HAYDON.
LAURETTE ...	...	Miss COLEMAN.
RAVINA (a Captive Victim of Grindoff)	...	Mrs. POYNTER.
*ZARA (the Zingara Chief's Daughter)	...	Miss LOUISE LECLERCQ.

* These Characters are introduced by Mr. Buckstone, and may advantageously be dispensed with on ordinary occasions.

ACT ONE.

DISTANT VIEW OF A MILL ON THE ELBE, BOHEMIA,

WITH COTTAGE OF KELMAR.

Round—"When the Wind Blows."

BORDERS OF THE FOREST.

INTERIOR OF KELMAR'S COTTAGE.

Sestette—"Stay, Pr'ythee, Stay."

THE FOREST.

INTERIOR OF ROBBER'S CAVE BENEATH THE MILL.

Chorus—"Fill, Boys, and Drink about," and "Now to the Forest We Repair."

DANCE OF ZINGARI,

By Louise Leclercq, Arthur Leclercq, and the Corps de Ballet.

ACT TWO.

INTERIOR OF KELMAR'S COTTAGE.

THE FOREST. A CAVE, WITH POWDER MAGAZINE. "THE FLASK" INN.

THE MILL.

THE EXPLOSION AND DESTRUCTION OF THE ROBBER BAND!

As originally performed at the Theatre Royal, Covent Garden. on October 21st, 1813.

GRINDOFF (*the Miller*) .... Mr. FARLEY.

COUNT FREDERICK FRIBERG .... Mr. VINING.

KARL (*his Servant*) .... Mr. LISTON.

LOTHAIR (*a young Peasant*) .... Mr. ABBOTT.

KELMAR (*an old Cottager*) .... Mr. CHAPMAN.

KRUITZ (*his Son*) .... MAST. GLADSTANES.

RIBER
GOLOTZ } (*Banditti*) .... { Mr. JEFFRIES.
ZINGRA   Mr. KING.
                                                   Mr. SLADER.

CLAUDINE
LAURETTE } (*Kelmar's Daughters*) ...... { Miss BOOTH
                                              Miss CAREW.

RAVINA .... Mrs. EGERTON.

The Miller's Men, Banditti, Officers of Count Friberg, &c.

Scenery.

ACT I.

SCENE 1.—River's bank. Sunset. Four rows of set owaters; ground-pieces, R. to L.; set rock, with working mill, 6th groove, L. C. Small working figures to appear on rock, with bags of flour; small boat to come from cavern beneath mill, and off R., then cross to L.; large boat to come on, L., twice. Landing bank in centre, front of ground-piece. Set cottage. R., (door practical) and lattice window.

SCENE 2.—Rocky glen, 1st groove, whalebone cut, L. C., to open and close, backed by dark piece.

SCENE 3.—Interior of cottage, 3rd groove. Set fireplace, R. 3 E. Door in flat, R. C, practical, backed with dark wood. Window, L. C., practical. Set staircase, practical, L. 3 E.

SCENE 4.—Rocky glen, (as before) 1st groove.

SCENE 5.—Cave, 4th and 5th grooves, opening in upper part of flat, R. C., with steps and platforms to descend, masked in by rocks; platforms, and steps behind opening, R. C., backed by close cave. Set rock, R. 3 E., with board on it painted "*Powder Magazine.*" Rock, L. 4 E., with a lighted lamp from roof. Trap door, R. C., practical, and steps beneath, practical.

ACT II.

SCENE 1.—Same as Scene 3. 3rd groove.
SCENE 2.—Same as Scene 4. 4th groove.
SCENE 3.—Same as Scene 5. 4th and 5th grooves.
SCENE 4.—Cottage flats, 1st groove. Sign of "Flask" over door, R. door in flat, R. C., practical, and window, L. flat, backed with hut interior.
SCENE 5.—Rocky water landscape, 7th groove. Set waters, groundpieces, set mill, L. 3 E. (to blow up into fragments) draw-bridge and portcullis, practical, from stage to mill; door in mill, practical.

Properties.

ACT I.

SCENE 1.—Six meal bags (full) brought from boat, L.; oars in boat. Some flour for millers. Small handle basket, covered with white cloth for Claudine. Pistols and daggers for Golotz and Riber.
SCENE 2.—Portmanteau, name of "Friberg" on it in brass nails, for Karl. Lightning and Rain.
SCENE 3.—Fire burning in fireplace, R. 3 E. Poker and shovel at fire. Table in centre, covered with white cloth; on it three plates, three knives and forks, plate of bread and cheese, bottle of wine, three glasses, two lighted candles in flat candlesticks. Three rustic chairs round table. Stool at fireplace, R. Basket of apples ready, L. 3 E., for Claudine. Poniard and sheath for Grindoff. Lightning, door flat, and window.
SCENE 4.—Dark handkerchief for Riber.
SCENE 5.—Old table in C.; on it three bottles of wine and twelve tin cups. Two benches and six stools on; Miller's frock, and slouched hat on wing, 2nd groove, L. Ten muskets on; daggers and pistols for robbers. Sword, daggers, and pistols for Grindoff. Dark lantern on, L. 3 E. Swords, pistols, and guns on flat, L.

ACT II.

SCENE 1.—Plain table on centre. Three rustic chairs on. Count's sword on table. Stool at fire, R.; very little fire burning, R. 3 E., in fireplace. Dark lantern lighted, and pistol, sure to fire, for Riber. Dagger for Karl.
SCENE 2.—Same as Scene 5, Act I. Coil of small black line for Lothair. Vial (labelled poison) for Ravina. Phosphorus bottle and matches for Lothair. Miller's hat on wing, L.
SCENE 3.—Flask for Karl. Two pistols for Wolf, sure fire, R. Bone of roast beef, for Karl, R. door in flat.
SCENE 4.—Slow match laid from stage in C. to mill. Lighted torch for Ravina. Red fire and explosion, L. 3 E. Wood crash, L. 3 E. Six stuffed figures of robbers behind mill, L. Guns, swords, and belts for hussars. Disguise cloak, for Lothair. Fighting swords for Lothair and Wolf.

Costumes.

FRIBERG.—Hussar uniform, red tights, red jacket, blue pelisse, richly laced with gold, and brown fur shako.

LOTHAIR.—*First Dress*: Light blue jacket, black tights, pantaloons, half boots, and broad-brimmed hat. *Second Dress*: Same style, in rags, and long hair, drapery. *Third Dress*: Green coat, green apron. *Fourth Dress*: Large cloak.

KELMAR.—Brown jerkin, bound with fur, gray tights, russet shoes, and gray wig.

KREUTZ.—Peasant boy; same as Lothair.

KARL.—The same uniform as Friberg; worsted lace, as a private hussar.

GRINDOFF.—*First Dress*: Light drab tunic, to cover all. *Second Dress*: red tunic, brown and black, open in the front, steel breastplate beneath, black tight pantaloons, conical hat, no rim, eagle feather, black ankle boots.

RIBER.—Brown jacket, hat, and feather, straight, same as Grindoff.

GOLOTZ.—Black, same as Riber, hat, &c.

1ST ROBBER.—Same as Grindoff.

2ND ROBBER.—Ditto.

TWELVE ROBBERS.—Same Bohemian costume, various colours.

SIX MILLER'S MEN.—Short smock frocks, white tights, and slouched hats.

THREE MILLER'S MEN.—(Chorus)—change from miller's men to robbers.

TWELVE HUSSARS.—Same as Karl.

CLAUDINE.—Neat peasant's dress.

RAVINA.—Brown slashed shirt, trimmed with black, two brass clasps to sashes, red petticoat showing through.

LAURETTA.—Neat peasant's dress.

Geo H Coveney

THE MILLER AND HIS MEN.

1816

ACT I.

SCENE FIRST.—*The Banks of a River. On the right, in the distance, a rocky eminence, on which is a windmill at work—a cottage in front,* R. 2 E.*—Sunset.*

Music.—The Miller's MEN *are seen in perspective, descending the eminence—they cross the river in boats, and land near the cottage, with their sacks, singing the following*

Round.

When the wind blows,
 When the mill goes,
Our hearts are all light and merry;
 When the wind drops,
 When the mill stops,
We drink and sing, hey down derry.
 Exeunt, two in the boat, R. U. E., *the rest,* R.

Enter KELMAR, *from the cottage,* R. 2 E.

KELM. What! more sacks, more grist to the mill! early and late the miller thrives : he that was my tenant is now my landlord; this hovel, that once sheltered him, is now the only dwelling of bankrupt broken-hearted Kelmar—well, I strove my best against misfortune, and, thanks be to heaven, have fallen respected, even by my enemies.

Enter CLAUDINE, *with a basket,* L. 2 E.

So, Claudine, you are returned. Where stayed you so long?

CLAUD. I was obliged to wait ere I could cross the ferry—there were other passengers.

KELM. (R. C.) Amongst whom I suppose was one in whose company time flew so fast—the sun had set before you had observed it.

CLAUD. (L. C.) No, indeed, father : since you desired me not to meet Lothair—and I told him what you had desired—I have never seen him but in the cottage here, when you were present.

KELM. You are a good girl—a dutiful child, and I believe you—you never yet deceived me.

CLAUD. Nor ever will, dear father—but——

KELM. But what?

CLAUD. I—I find it very lonely passing the borders of the forest without—without——

KELM. Without Lothair.

CLAUD. You know, 'tis dangerous, father.

KELM. Not half so dangerous as love—subdue it, child, in time.

CLAUD. But the robbers?

KELM. Robbers! what then?—they cannot injure thee or thy father—alas! we have no more to lose—yet thou hast one treasure left, innocence!—guard well thy heart, for should the fatal passion there take root, 'twill rob thee of thy peace.

CLAUD. You told me, once, love's impulse could not be resisted.

KELM. When the object is worthless, it should not be indulged.

CLAUD. Is Lothair worthless?

KELM. No ; but he is poor, almost as you are.

CLAUD. Do riches without love give happiness?

KELM. Never.

CLAUD. Then I must be unhappy if I wed the miller Grindoff.

KELM. Not so—not so ;—independence gives comfort, but love without competence is endless misery. You can never wed Lothair.

CLAUD. (*sighing*) I can never love the miller.

KELM. Then you shall never marry him—though to see you Grindoff's wife be the last wish of your old father's heart. Go in, child; go in, Claudine. (CLAUDINE *kisses his hand, and exit into cottage,* R. 2 E.) 'Tis plain her heart is rivetted to Lothair, and honest Grindoff yet must sue in vain.

Enter LOTHAIR, *hastily.* L. 2 E.

LOTH. Ah! Kelmar, and alone!—where is Claudine?

KELM. At home, in her father's house—where should she be?

LOTH. Then she has escaped—she is safe, and I am happy—I did not accompany her in vain.

KELM. Accompany!—accompany!—has she then told me a falsehood? Were you with her, Lothair?

LOTH. No—ye—yes. (*aside*) I must not alarm him.

KELM. (R.) What mean these contradictions?

LOTH. She knew not I was near her—you have denied our meeting, but you cannot prevent my loving her—I have watched her daily through the village and along the borders of the forest.

KELM. I thank you; but she needs no guard; her poverty will protect her from a thief.

LOTH. (L.) Will her beauty protect her from a libertine?

KELM. Her virtue will.

LOTH. I doubt it:—what can her resistance avail against the powerful arm of villany?

KELM. Is there such a wretch?

LOTH. There is.

KELM. Lothair, Lothair! I fear you glance at the miller Grindoff. This is not well; this is not just.

LOTH. Kelmar, you wrong me; 'tis true, he is my enemy, for he bars my road to happiness. Yet I respect his character; the riches that industry has gained him he employs in assisting the unfortunate—he has protected you and your child, and I honour him.

KELM. If not to Grindoff, to whom did you allude?

LOTH. Listen:—as I crossed the hollow way in the forest, I heard a rustling in the copse. Claudine had reached the bank above. As I was following, voices, subdued and whispering, struck my ear. Her name was distinctly pronounced: "She comes," said one; "Now! now we may secure her," cried the second; and instantly two men advanced; a sudden exclamation burst from my lips, and arrested their intent; they turned to seek me, and with dreadful imprecations vowed death to the intruder. Stretched beneath a bush of holly, I lay concealed; they passed within my reach; I scarely breathed, while I observed them to be ruffians, uncouth and savage—they were banditti.

KELM. Banditti! Are they not yet content? All that I had—all that the hand of Providence had spared, they have deprived me of; and would they take my child?

LOTH. 'Tis plain they would. Now, Kelmar, hear the last proposal of him you have rejected. Without Claudine my life is but a blank—useless to others and wretched to myself; it shall be risked to avenge the wrongs you have suffered. I'll seek these robbers! if I should fall, your daughter will more readily obey your wish, and become the wife of Grindoff. If I should succeed, promise her to me. The reward I shall receive will secure our future comfort, and thus your fears and your objections both are satisfied.

KELM. (*affected*) Lothair, thou art a good lad, a noble lad, and worthy my daughter's love; she had been freely thine, but that by sad experience I know how keen the pangs of penury are to a parent's heart. My sorrows may descend to her when I am gone, but I have nothing to bequeath her else.

LOTH. Then you consent?

KELM. I do, I do; but pray be careful. I fear 'tis a rash attempt: you must have help.

LOTH. Then, indeed, I fail as others have before me. No, Kelmar, I must go alone, pennyless, unarmed, and secretly. None but yourself must know my purpose, or my person.

KELM. Be it as you will; but pray be careful; come, thou shalt see her.   (*the mill stops*)

LOTH. I'll follow; it may be my last farewell.

KELM. Come in—I see the mill has stopped. Grindoff will be here anon; he always visits me at nightfall, when labour ceases. Come.

                    Exit KELMAR *into the cottage* R. 2 E.

LOTH. Yes, at the peril of my life, I'll seek them. With the juice of herbs my face shall be discoloured, and, in the garb of misery, I'll throw myself within their power

—the rest I leave to Providence. (*Music*) But the miller comes.

Exit to the cottage, R. 2 E.—the Miller appears in perspective coming from the crag in the rock—the boat disappears on the opposite side.

Enter the two Robbers, RIBER and GOLOTZ, hastily, R. 2 E. —they rush up to the cottage, L. 2 E., and peep in at the window.

RIBER. (*retiring from the window*) We are too late— she has reached the cottage.

GOL. Curse on the interruption that detained us; we shall be rated for this failure.

RIBER. (R.) Hush! not so loud. (*goes again cautiously to the window of the cottage*) Ha! Lothair.

GOL. (L.) Lothair! 'twas he, then, that marred our purpose; he shall smart for't.

RIBER. Back! back! he comes. On his return he dies; he cannot pass us both.

Music—They retire behind a tree, L. U. E.—a boat passed in the distance from the mouth of the cavern in the rock beneath the mill, L. C. to R. U. E., then R. to L., then draws up to the bank.

Enter GRINDOFF, THE MILLER, in the boat, who jumps ashore, L.—Re-enter LOTHAIR, at the same moment, from the cottage, R. 2 E.

GRIN. (L., *disconcerted*) Lothair!

LOTH. (R.) Ay, my visit here displeases you, no doubt.

GRIN. Nay, we are rivals, but not enemies, I trust. We love the same girl; we strive the best we can to gain her; if you are fortunate, I'll wish you joy with all my heart; if I should have the luck on't, you'll do the same by me, I hope.

LOTH. You have little fear; I am poor, you are rich. He needn't look far that would see the end on't.

GRIN. But you are young and likely. I am honest and rough; the chances are as much yours as mine.

LOTH. Well, time will show. I bear you no enmity. Farewell! (*crosses to L.*)

GRIN. (R., *aside*) He must not pass the forest. (*to* LO-THAIR) Whither go you?

LOTH. (L.) To the village; I must haste, or 'twill be late ere I reach the ferry.   (*it begins to grow dark*)

RIBER. (*who with* GOLOTZ *is watching them from* L. U. E.) He will escape us yet.

GRIN. (L. C.) Stay, my boat shall put you across the river. Besides, the evening looks stormy—come, it will save your journey half a league.

RIBER. (*aside,* L. U. E.) It will save his life.

LOTH. Well, I accept your offer, and I thank you.

GRIN. Your hand.

LOTH. Farewell!

(he goes into the boat, and pushes off, L.)

GRIN. So, I am rid of him; if he had met Claudine!—but she is safe—now, then, for Kelmar.

Exit into the cottage, L. 2 E.

Re-enter RIBER *and* GOLOTZ, L. U. E.

RIBER. Curse on this chance! we have lost him!

GOL. But a time may come.

RIBER. A time shall come, and shortly, too.

Exeunt, L. 2 E.

SCENE SECOND.—*The Forest—distant thunder—stage dark.*

Enter KARL, *dragging after him a portmanteau,* L.

KARL. Here's a pretty mess! here's a precious spot of work!—Pleasant upon my soul—lost in a labyrinth, without love or liquor—the sun gone down, a storm got up, and no getting out of this vile forest, turn which way you will.

COUNT. (*calling without,* L.) Halloo! Karl! Karl!

KARL. Ah, you may call and bawl, master of mine; you'll not disturb anything here but a wild boar or two, and a wolf, perhaps.

Enter COUNT FREDERICK FRIBERG, L.

COUNT. Karl, where are you?

KARL. (R.) Where am I! that's what I want to know —this cursed wood has a thousand turnings, and not one that turns right.

COUNT. (L.) Careless coxcomb! said you not you could remember the track?

KARL. So I should, sir, if I could find the path—but trees will grow, and since I was here last, the place has got so bushy and briery, that—that I have lost my way.

COUNT. You have lost your senses.

KARL. No, sir, I wish I had; unfortunately, my senses are all in the highest state of perfection.

COUNT. Why not use them to more effect?

KARL. I wish I'd the opportunity; my poor stomach cau testify that I taste——

COUNT. What?

KARL. Nothing; it's as empty as my head: but I see danger, smell a tempest, hear the cry of wild beasts, and feel——

COUNT. How?

KARL. Particularly unpleasant. (*thunder and rain*) Oh, we are in for it: do you hear, sir?

COUNT. We must be near the river; could we but reach the ferry, 'tis but a short league to the Chateau Friberg. (*crosses*, R.)

KARL. (R.) Ah, sir, I wish we were there, and I seated in the old arm-chair in the servant's hall, talking of— holloa!

COUNT. (L.) What now?

KARL. I felt a spot of rain on my nose as big as a bullet. (*thunder and rain*) There, there, it's coming on again— seek some shelter, sir; some hollow tree, whilst I, for my sins, endeavour once more to find the way, and endure another curry-combing among these cursed brambles. Come sir. (*the storm increases*) Lor', how it rumbles— this way, sir—this way.   *Exeunt*, R.

SCENE THIRD.—*A Room in the Cottage—a door*, R. *flat— a window*, L. *flat—a fire*, R. 2 E.—*tables*, R. *and* L.— *chairs*, &c.

GRINDOFF, L., *and* KELMAR, R., *discovered sitting at the table*, R.—*thunder and rain*.

KELM. 'Tis a rough night, miller: the thunder roars, and, by the murmuring of the flood, the mountain torrents have descended. Poor Lothair! he'll scarcely have crossed the ferry.

GRIN. Lothair by this is safe at home, old friend; before the storm commenced I passed him in my boat across the river. (*aside*) He seems less anxious for his daughter than for this bold stripling.

KELM. Worthy man! you'll be rewarded for all such deeds hereafter. Thank heaven, Claudine is safe! Hark!
(*thunder heard*)

GRIN. (*aside*) She is safe by this time, or I am much mistaken.

KELM. She will be here anon.

GRIN. (*aside*) I doubt that. (*to* KELMAR) Come, here's to her health, old Kelmar—, would I could once call you father!

KELM. You may do soon; but even your protection would now, I fear, be insufficient to——

GRIN. What mean you? Insufficient!

KELM. The robbers—this evening in the forest——

GRIN. (*rising*) Ha!

KELM. (*rising*) Did not Lothair, then, tell you?

GRIN. Lothair?

KELM. Yes; but all's well; be not alarmed—see, she is here.

GRIN. Here!

Enter CLAUDINE, R.—GRINDOFF *endeavours to suppress his surprise.*

GRIN. Claudine! Curse on them both!

KELM. (C.) Both! how knew you there were two?

GRIN. (L.) 'Sdeath!—you—you said robbers, did you not? They never have appeared singly; therefore, I thought you meant two.

KELM. You are right. But for Lothair they had deprived me of my child.

GRIN. How!—Did Lothair? Humph! he's a courageous youth.

CLAUD. That he is; but he's gentle, too. What has happened?

KELM. Nothing, child, nothing. (*aside to* GRINDOFF)

Do not speak on't, 'twill terrify her.   Come, Claudine,
now for supper.   What have you brought us ?

CLAUD. Thanks to the miller's bounty, plenty.

KELM. The storm increases !

KARL. (*calling without,* R. *door flat*) Holloa ! holloa !

KELM. And hark !   I hear a voice—listen !

KARL. (*calling again without,* R. *door flat*) Holloa !

CLAUD. The cry of some bewildered traveller.

(*the cry repeated, and a violent knock at the door,* R. *flat*)

KELM. Open the door.

GRIN. Not so; it may be dangerous.

KELM. Danger comes in silence and in secret; my door
was never shut against the wretched while I knew pros-
perity, nor shall it be closed now to my fellows in
misfortune.   (*to* CLAUDINE) Open the door, I say.

(*the knock is repeated, and* CLAUDINE *opens the door*)

Enter KARL, R. *door flat, with a portmanteau.*

KARL. (C.) Why, in the name of dark nights and
tempests, didn't you open the door at first?   Have you
no charity ?

KELM. (R. C.) In our hearts plenty, in our gift but little ;
yet all we have is yours.

KARL. Then I'll share all you have with my master;
thank you, old gentleman; you won't fare the worse for
sheltering honest Karl and Count Frederick Friberg.

GRIN. (L.) Friberg!

KARL. Ay, I'll soon fetch him; he's waiting now,
looking as melancholy as a mourning coach in a snow-
storm, at the foot of a tree, wet as a drowned rat; so stir
up the fire, bless you! clap on the kettle, give us the best
eatables and drinkables you have, a clean table-cloth, a
couple of warm beds, and don't stand upon ceremony;
we'll accept every civility and comfort you can bestow
upon us without scruple.

(*throws down the portmanteau,* C., *and exit,* R. *door flat*)

GRIN. (L.) Friberg, did he say ?

CLAUD. (R.) 'Tis the young count, so long expected.

KELM. (R. C.) Can it be possible? without attendants,
and at such a time, too ?

GRIN. (*looking at the portmanteau, on which is the name in brass nails*) It must be the same!—Kelmar, good night.   (*going up towards the door*)

KELM. Nay, not yet—the storm rages.

GRIN. I fear it may increase; besides, your visitors may not like my company; good night.

Enter COUNT FREDERICK FRIBERG, R. *door flat, jollowed by* KARL—*he stops suddenly, and eyes the* MILLER, *as if recollecting him—*GRINDOFF *appears to avoid his scrutiny.*

COUNT. (C.) Your kindness is well timed; we might have perished; accept my thanks. (*aside*) I should know that face.

GRIN. (L.) To me your thanks are not due.

COUNT. That voice, too!

GRIN. This house is Kelmar's.

    (KARL *places the portmanteau on the table,* L. U. E.)

COUNT. Kelmar's!

KELM. (R. C) Ay, my dear master; my fortunes have deserted me, but my attachment to your family still remains.

COUNT. Worthy old man. How happens this: the richest tenant of my late father's land—the honest, the faithful Kelmar, in a hovel?

KELM. It will chill your hearts to hear.

KARL. (*at the fire, drying and warming himself*) Then don't tell us, pray, for our bodies are cramped with cold already.

KELM. 'Tis a terrible tale.

KARL (*advancing,* L. C.) Then, for the love of a good appetite and a dry skin, don't tell it, for I've been terrified enough in the forest to-night to last me my life.

COUNT. Be silent, Karl. (*retires to fire with* KELMAR)

GRIN. (L.) In—in the forest?

KARL. (L. C.) Ay.

GRIN. What should alarm you there?

KARL. What should alarm me there? come, that's a good one. Why, first, I lost my way; trying to find that, I lost the horses; then I tumbled into a quagmire, and nearly lost my life.

GRIN. Psha! this is of no consequence.

KARL. Isn't it?   I have endured more hardships since morning than a knight-errant.   My head's broken, my body's bruised, and my joints are dislocated.   I hav'nt three square inches about me but what are scarified with briers and brambles ; and, above all, I have not tasted a morsel of food since sunrise.   Egad! instead of my making a meal of anything, I've been in constant expectation of the wolves making a meal of me.

GRIN. Is this all?

KARL. All!—No, it's not all; pretty well, too, I think. When I recovered the path, I met two polite gentlemen with long knives in their hands.

GRIN. Hey !

KARL. And because I refused a kind invitation of theirs, they were affronted, and were just on the point of ending all my troubles when up came my master.

GRIN. Well !

KARL. Well! yes, it was well indeed, for after a struggle they made off; one of them left his sting behind, though ; look, here's a poker to stir up a man's courage with ! (*showing a poniard*)

GRIN. A poniard !

KARL. Ay.

GRIN. (*snatching at it*) Give it me.

KARL. (*retaining the dagger*) For what?   It's lawful spoil—didn't I win it in battle?   No! I'll keep it as a trophy of my victory.

(*during this time,* KELMAR *and* CLAUDINE *have taken and hung up the Count's cloak, handed him a chair, and are conversing*)

GRIN. It will be safer in my possession : it may lead to a discovery of him who wore it—and——

KARL. It may—you are right—therefore I'll deliver it into the hands of Count Frederick : he'll soon ferret the rascals out; set a reward on their heads—five thousand crowns, dead or alive! that's the way to manœuvre 'em. (*poking* GRINDOFF *in the ribs*)

GRIN. Indeed! humph! (*turns up,* L.)

KARL. Humph! don't half like that chap—never saw such a ferocious black muzzle in my life—that miller's a rogue in grain.

Count. (*advancing*, c.) Nay, nay, speak of it no more. I will not take an old man's bed to ease my youthful limbs; I have slept soundly on a ruder couch—and that chair shall be my resting-place.

Claud. (R.) The miller's man, Riber, perhaps can entertain his excellency better;—he keeps the Flask here, on the hill, sir.

Grin. (L. C.) His house contains but one bed.

Karl. (L.) Only one?

Grin. And that is occupied.

Karl. The devil it is!

Count. It matters not; I am contented here.

Karl. That's more than I am. (*retires up*, L.)

Grin. But stay : perchance his guest has left it; if so, 'tis at Count Frederick's service. I'll go directly and bring you word. (*aside*) I may now prevent surprise—the storm has ceased; I will return immediately.

    (*unseen he drops the sheath of a dagger*, L. C., *and exit*, R. D. F.)

Count. (*eagerly*) Kelmar, tell me, who is that man?

Kelmar. (*advancing*) The richest tenant, sir, you have; what Kelmar was when you departed from Bohemia, Grindoff now is.

Count. Grindoff!—I remember, in my youth, a favoured servant of my father's, who resembled him in countenance and voice—the recollection is strong upon my memory, but I hope deceives me, for he was a villain who betrayed his trust.

Kelm. (R. C.) I have heard the circumstance; it happened just before I entered your good father's service—his name was Wolf.

Count. The same.

Karl. (L.) And if this is not the same, I suspect he is a very near relation.

Kelm. (*angrily*) Nay, sir, you mistake—Grindoff is my friend.—Come, Claudine, is all ready?

Karl. Oh, it's a sore subject, is it?

                    Exeunt Kelmar *and* Claudine, R.

Your friend, is he, old gentleman?—Sir—sir——

Count. (*who has become thoughtful*) Well! what say you?

KARL. I don't like our quarters, sir; we are in a bad neighbourhood.

COUNT. (R.) I fear we are; Kelmar's extreme poverty may have tempted him to league with—yet his daughter?

KARL. (L.) His daughter—a decoy!—nothing but a trap; don't believe her sir; we are betrayed, murdered, if we stay here. I'll endure anything, everything, if you will but depart, sir. Dark nights, bad roads, hail, rain, assassins, and—hey! what's this? (*sees and picks up the scabbard dropped by Grindoff*) Oh, Lord, what's the matter with me? My mind misgives me; and here—(*he sheathes the dagger in it and finds it fit*) fits to a hair—we are in the lion's den!

COUNT. 'Tis evident, we are snared, caught.

KARL. O, lord! don't say so.

Re-enter KELMAR *and* CLAUDINE, *followed by* LAURETTE *and* KRUITZ *with supper things, &c.,* R.

KELM. Come, come, youngsters, bestir—spread the cloth, and——

COUNT. Kelmar, I have bethought me; at every peril, I must on to-night.

KELM. To-night!

CLAUD. Not to-night, I beseech you; you know not half your danger. (*goes to the table,* L., *and places her hand carelessly on the portmanteau*)

KARL. Danger! (*aside*) Cockatrice! (*to* CLAUDINE) I'll thank you for that portmanteau.

COUNT. Let it remain—it may be an object to them, 'tis none to me,—it will be safer here with honest Kelmar.

KELM. But why so sudden?

KARL. My master has recollected something that must be done to-night—or to-morrow it may be out of his power.

CLAUD. (R.) Stay till the miller returns.

KARL. Till he returns! (*aside*) Ah, the fellow's gone to get assistance, and if he comes before we escape, we shall be cut and hashed to mince-meat.

COUNT. Away!   (*advancing to the door*)

Enter GRINDOFF, *suddenly,* R. D. F.

KARL. (L.) It's all over with us.

KELM. (R. C.) Well, friend, what success?

GRIN. (C.) Bad enough—the count must remain here.

COUNT. (L. C.) Must remain!

GRIN. There is no resource.

KARL. I thought so.

GRIN. To-morrow, Riber can dispose of you both.

KARL. Dispose of us! (*aside*) Ay, put us to bed with a spade—that fellow's a grave-digger.

COUNT. Then I must cross the ford to-night.

GRIN. Impossible; the torrent has swept the ferry barge from the shore, and driven it down the stream.

COUNT. Perhaps, your boat——

GRIN. Mine! 'twould be madness to resist the current now—and in the dark, too.

COUNT. What reward may tempt you?

GRIN. Not all you are worth, sir, until to-morrow.

KARL. To-morrow!—(*aside*) Ah! we are crow's meat, to a certainty.

GRIN. (*aside, looking askance around the room*) All is right: they have got the scabbard, and their suspicions now must fall on Kelmar.

Exit GRINDOFF, R. D. F., *bidding them all good night.*

COUNT. Well, we must submit to circumstances. (*aside to* KARL) Do not appear alarmed; when all is still, we may escape.

KARL. Why not now? There are only two of 'em.

COUNT. There may be others near.

Sestette.

CLAUD.   Stay, prithee, stay—the night is dark,
          The cold wind whistles—hark! hark! hark!

COUNT. } (*together*) { We must away.
KARL. }   { Pray, come away.

CLAUD.   The night is dark,
          The cold wind whistles.

ALL.   Hark! hark! hark!

CLAUD.   Stay, prithee, stay—the way is lone,
          The ford is deep—the boat is gone.

KELM.   And mountain torrents swell the flood,
          And robbers lurk within the wood.

ALL.   Here $\left\{\begin{array}{c}\text{you}\\\text{we}\end{array}\right\}$ must stay till morning bright
Breaks through the dark and dismal night,
And merry sings the rising lark,
And hush'd the night bird—hark! hark! hark!
(CLAUDINE *tenderly detains the* COUNT—KELMAR
detains KARL—*tableau closed in by*)

SCENE FOURTH.—*The Depth of the Forest—stage dark.*

Enter LOTHAIR, L., *with his dress and complexion entirely
changed; his appearance is extremely wretched.*

LOTH. This way, this—in the moaning of the blast, at
intervals, I heard the tread of feet—and as the moon's
light burst from the stormy clouds, I saw two figures
glide like departed spirits to this deep glen. Now,
heaven prosper me, for my attempt is desperate! (*looking
off*, R.) ah, they come!   (*retires*, R. 2 E.)

Music.—Enter RIBER, R., GOLOTZ *follows: they look
around cautiously, then advance to a particular rock,
L. C., which is nearly concealed by underwood and roots
of trees.*

LOTH. (*advancing*, R.) Hold! (*the* ROBBERS *start, and
eye him with ferocious surprise*) So, my purpose is accomplished—at last I have discovered you.

RIBER. (*crosses*, C.) Indeed! it will cost you dear.

LOTH. It has already—I have been hunted through
the country; but now my life is safe.

RIBER. Safe!

LOTH. Ay, is it not? Would you destroy a comrade?
Look at me, search me—I am unarmed, defenceless!

GOLOT. Why come you hither?

LOTH. To join your brave band—the terror of Bohemia.

RIBER. How knew you our retreat?

LOTH. No matter. In the service of Count Friberg I
have been disgraced—and fly from punishment to seek
revenge.

GOLOT. (*to* RIBER) How say you?

LOTH. (*aside*) They hesitate—the young Count is far

from home, and his name I may use without danger. (*to the* ROBBERS) Lead me to your chief.

RIBER. We will — not so fast; your sight must be concealed. (*offering to bind his forehead*)

LOTH. Ah! (*hesitates*) May I trust you?

GOLOT. Do you doubt?

RIBER. Might we not despatch you as you are?

LOTH. Enough; bind me, and lead on.

(*Music.—They conceal his sight, take each a hand, and lead* LOTHAIR *round the stage, interposing their swords to cause him to raise his feet and stoop his head, so that he may have no idea of their path* —GOLOTZ *leads* LOTHAIR *to the rock, L., pushes the brushwood aside, and both exeunt, followed by* RIBER, *watching that they are not observed*)

SCENE FIFTH.—*A Cavern.*

BANDITTI *discovered variously employed, chiefly sitting carousing around tables on which are flasks of wine, &c. —steps rudely cut in the rock, in the background, lead-ing to an elevated recess, C., on which is inscribed:* "Powder Magazine"—*other steps leading to an opening in the cave—a grated door, R.—stage light.*

Chorus.—BANDITTI.

Fill, boys, and drink about,—
Wine will banish sorrow;
Come, drain the goblet out,
We'll have more to-morrow.

(*the* ROBBERS *all rise and come forward*)

Slow Movement.

We live free from fear,
In harmony here,
Combin'd, just like brother and brother;
And this be our toast,
The free-booter's boast,
Success and good-will to each other!
Fill, boys, &c.

Chorus.

Enter RAVINA, *through the grated door,* R., *as th*
conclude.

RAVINA. What, carousing yet—sotting yet!

ZINGRA. How now, Ravina; why so churlish?

RAVINA. To sleep, I say—or wait upon yourselves. I'll stay no longer from my couch to please you. Is it not enough that I toil from daybreak, bnt you must disturb me ever with your midnight revelry?

ZINGRA. (R. C.) You were not wont to be so savage, woman.

RAVINA. Nor you so insolent. Look, you repent it not!

1ST ROBBER. (L. C.) Psha! heed her no more. Jealousy hath soured her.

ZINGRA. I forgive her railing.

RAVINA. Forgive!

ZINGRA. Ay! our leader seeks another mistress! and 'tis rather hard upon thee, I confess, after five year's captivity, hard service too, and now that you are accustomed to our way of life—we pity thee.

RAVINA. Pity me! I am indeed an object of compassion: five long years a captive, hopeless still of liberty. Habit has almost made my heart cold as these rude rocks that screen me from the light of heaven. Miserable lost Ravina! by dire necessity become an agent in their wickedness, yet I pine for virtue and for freedom.

ZINGRA. Leave us to our wine. Come, boys, fill all, fiil full, "to our captain's bride."

ROBBERS. To our captain's bride!

(*a single note on the bugle is heard from below,* R. C.)

ZINGRA. Hark! 'tis from the lower cave. (*bugle note repeated*) She comes! Ravina, look you receive her as becomes the companion of our chief—remember!

RAVINA. I shall remember. (*crosses,* L.) So, another victim to hypocrisy and guilt. Poor wretch! she loves perhaps, as I did, the miller Grindoff; but, as I do, may live to execrate the outlaw and the robber!

(*Music—the trap in the floor is thrown open*)

Enter RIBER, *through the floor, followed by* GOLOTZ *and* LOTHAIR—*they all advance,* R.

ROBBERS. Hail to our new companion!

RAVINA. (L.) A man!

(LOTHAIR *tears the bandage from his eyes as he arrives in the cave—the* ROBBERS *start back on perceiving a man*)

LOTH. Thanks for your welcome!

ZINGRA. Who have we here?—Speak!

RIBER. A recruit. Where is the captain?

ZINGRA. Where is the captain's bride?

RIBER. Of her hereafter. (*a bugle is heard above,* L. U. E.)

ROBBERS. Wolf! Wolf!

Enter GRINDOFF, *in robber's apparel*—*he descends the opening, and advances,* C.

ZINGRA.   }   Welcome, noble captain!
ROBBERS. }

GRIN. (*starts at seeing* LOTHAIR, R.) A stranger!

LOTH. (*aside*) Grindoff!

      (*the* ROBBERS *lay hands on their swords, &c.*)

GRIN. Ha! betrayed! Who has done this?

RIBER. (*advancing,* L. C.) I brought him hither, to——

GRIN. Riber! humph! You have executed my orders well, have you not? Where is Claudine?

LOTH. (R.) Claudine! (*aside*) Villain! hyprocrite!

GRIN. Know you Claudine, likewise?

RIBER. She escaped us in the forest. Some meddling fool thwarted our intent, and——

GRIN. Silence, I know it all; a word with you presently. Now, stranger—(*crossing to* LOTHAIR) but I mistake; we should be old acquaintance—my name is so familiar to you. What is your purpose here?

LOTH. Revenge!

GRIN. On whom?

LOTH. On one whose cruelty and oppression well deserve it.

GRIN. His name?

LOTH. (*aside*) Would I dare mention it!

GRIN. His name, I say?

RIBER. He complains of Count Friberg.

GRIN. Indeed! then your purpose will soon be accomplished: he arrived this night, and shelters at old Kelmar's cottage; he shall never pass the river; should he once reach the Chateau Friberg, it would be fatal to our band.

LOTH. Arrived! (*aside*) What have I done! My fatal indiscretion has destroyed him. (*to* GRINDOFF) Let him fall by my hand.

GRIN. It may tremble—it trembles now. The firmest of our band have failed. (*looking at* RIBER) Henceforth the enterprize shall be my own.

LOTH. Let me accompany you.

GRIN. Not to-night.

LOTH. To-night.

GRIN. Áy, before the dawn appears, he dies! Riber!
(LOTHAIR *clasps his hands in agony, and goes up—*
RIBER *advances,* L.)

RAVINA. (*advancing,* R.) What, more blood! must Friberg's life be added to the list?

GRIN. It must; our safety claims it.

RAVI. Short-sighted man! will not his death doubly arouse the sluggish arm of justice? The whole country, hitherto kept in awe by dissension and selfish fear, will join; reflect in time; beware their retribution!

GRIN. When I need a woman's help and counsel, I'll seek it of the compassionate Ravina. Begone! (*exit* RAVINA, R. *door*) Riber, I say!

RIBER. I await your orders.

GRIN. Look you execute them better than the last—look to't! The Count and his companion rest at Kelmar's; it must be done within an hour: arm, and attend me—at the same time I will secure Claudine—and should Kelmar's vigilance interpose to mar us, he henceforth shall be an inmate here.

LOTH. (R.) Oh, villain!

GRIN. (*rushing towards* LOTHAIR) How mean you?

LOTH. Friberg—let me go with you.

GRIN. You are too eager; I will not trust thy inexperience: trust you! what surety have we of your faith?

LOTH. My oath.

GRIN. Swear, then, never to desert the object, never

to betray the cause for which you sought our band—revenge on——

LOTH. On him who has deeply, basely injured me, I swear it.

GRIN. 'Tis well—your name?

LOTH. Spiller!

GRIF. (*to* RIBER) Quick! arm and attend me. (RIBER *retires*, R.) Are those sacks in the mill disposed of as I ordered?

ZINGRA. They are, captain.

GRIN. Return with the flour to-morrow, and be careful that all assume the calmness of industry and content. With such appearance, suspicion itself is blind; 'tis the safeguard of our band. Fill me a horn, and then to business. (*a* ROBBER *hands him a horn of wine; he drinks*) The Miller and his Men!

ROBBERS. (*drinking*) The Miller and his Men!

(GRINDOF *and* ROBBERS *laugh heartily*—GRINDOFF *puts on his miller's frock, hat, &c.*—RIBER, *armed with pistols in his belt, advances with a dark lantern, and exeunt with* GRINDOFF *through the rock,* L. F.)

Chorus.—BANDITTI.

Now to the forest we repair,
Awhile like spirits wander there;
In darkness we secure our prey,
And vanish at the dawn of day.

[A dance of Zingari Girls was introduced here. It was performed with much spirit by Miss Louise Leclercq and the Corps de Ballet.]

END OF ACT I.

ACT II.

SCENE FIRST.—*The Interior of Kelmar's Cottage, as before.*

COUNT FREDERICK FRIBERG *discovered asleep in a chair, reclining on a table near* L. 2 E., *and at the opposite side, near the fire,* KARL *is likewise seen asleep,* R.—*the Count's sword lies on the table,* L.—*the fire is nearly extinguished—stage dark—Music as the curtain rises. Enter* CLAUDINE, *with a lamp, down the stairs,* L 2 E.

CLAUD. All still, all silent! The Count and his companions are undisturbed! What can it mean? My father wanders from his bed, restless as myself. Alas! the infirmities of age and sorrow afflict him sorely. Night after night I thow myself upon a sleepless couch, ready to fly to his assistance, and—hush—hush! (CLAUDINE *extinguishes the light, and conceals herself,* L. 2 E.)

Enter KELMAR, R.

KELM. They sleep—sleep soundly—ere they wake, I may return from my inquiry. If Grindoff's story was correct, I still may trust him—still may the Count confide in him; but his behaviour last night, unusual and mysterious, hangs like a fearful dream upon my mind—his anxiety to leave the cottage, his agitation at the appearance of Count Friberg—but above all, his assertion that the ferry-barge was lost, disturbs me. My doubts shall soon be ended. At this lone hour I may pass the borders unperceived, and the gray dawn that now glimmers in the east will direct my path.

Looks about him fearful of disturbing the sleepers, and exit, R. *door in flat.*

CLAUD. (*advancing,* C.) My father appears unusually agitated. Ah, it may be! sometimes he wanders on the river's brink, watching the bright orb of day bursting from the dark trees, and breathes a prayer, a blessing for his child; yet 'tis early, very early—yet it may be—Oh, father, my dear—dear father! *Exit,* R. *door in flat.*

KARL. Yaw! (*snoring*) Damn the rats! Yaw, what a noise they keep up! Hey, where am I? Oh, in this infernal hovel; the night-mare has rode me into a jelly; then such horrible dreams, yaw! (*a light from the dark lantern borne by* RIBER *is seen passing the window,* L. *flat*) And such a swarm of rats—damn the rats! (*lays his hand on his poniard*) They'd better keep off, for I'm hungry enough to eat one. Bew—eu. (*shivering*) I wish it were morning. (*Music*)

Enter RIBER, R. *door in flat; he suddenly retires, observing a light occasioned by* KARL's *stirring the fire with his dagger.*

KARL. What's that? (*listens*) Nothing but odd noises

all night; wonder how my master can sleep for such a—yaw—aw! Damn the rats! (*lies down*)

> *Music—Enter* RIBER *cautiously,* R. *door in flat, holding forward the lantern—*GRINDOFF *follows.* RIBER, *on seeing the* COUNT, *draws a poniard—he raises his arm,* GRINDOFF *catches it, and prevents the blow. Appropriate music.*

GRIN. Not yet; first secure my prize, Claudine; these are safe.

KARL. How the varmint swarm!

GRIN. Hush! he dreams.

RIBER. It shall be his last.

KARL. Rats, rats!

RIBER. What says he?

KARL. Rats!—they all come from the mill.

RIBER. Do they so?

KARL. Ay, set traps for 'em, poison 'em.

> (RIBER, *again attempting to advance, is detained by* GRINDOFF)

GRIN. Again so rash—remember!

KARL.—I shall never forget that fellow in the forest.

RIBER. Ha! do you mark?

GRIN. Fear them not; be still till I return; he is sound; none sleep so hard as those that babble in their dreams. Stir not, I charge you; yet, should Kelmar—ay—should you hear a noise without, instantly despatch.

> *Exit* GRINDOFF, *up the stairs,* L. 2 E.

RIBER. Enough! (KARL *wakes again—he observes* RIBER, *grasps his dagger, and, watching the motion of the* ROBBER, *acts accordingly*) This delay is madness, but I must obey. (*looking at the priming of his pistol, then towards the table—*KARL *drops to his position*) Hey, a sword! (*advancing to the table,* L., *and removing the sword*) Now, all is safe—Hark! (*a noise without, as of something falling*) 'Tis time! if this should fail, my poniard will secure him.

> *Music—*RIBER *advances hastily, and, in the act of bringing his pistol to the level against the* COUNT, *is stabbed by* KARL, *who has arisen and closely followed his every movement; at the same moment,*

Enter GRINDOFF, L. 2 E.,—*the* COUNT, *rushing from the chair at the noise of the pistol, seizes him by the collar— the group stand amazed.—Tableau.*

COUNT. Speak! what means this?

KARL. (*advancing*) They've caught a tartar, sir, that's all. Hey, the miller!

GRIN. Ay!

COUNT. How came you here?

GRIN. (C.) To—to do you service.

COUNT. At such an hour!

GRIN. 'Tis never too late to do good.

COUNT. Good!

GRIN. Yes; you have been in danger.

KARL. Have we? Thank you for your news.

GRIN. You have been watched by the Banditti.

COUNT. So it appears.

KARL. But how did you know it?

GRIN. (*confused*) There is my proof. (*Pointing to the body of* RIBER)

KARL. But how the plague got you into the house?— Through a rat-hole?

COUNT. Explain.

GRIN. Few words will do that:—on my return to the mill, I found you might repose there better than in this house; at all events, I knew you would be safer in my care.

COUNT. Safer! Proceed! what mean you?

KARL. (*aside*) Safer!

GRIN. Kelmar——

COUNT. Hah!

GRIN. Had you no suspicion of him?—no mistrust of his wish to—to detain you?

COUNT. I confess, I——

GRIN. (*to* KARL) The poniard you obtained in the forest, that you refused to give me——

KARL. This?

GRIN. Is Kelmar's.

COUNT. Wretch!

KARL. I thought so; I found the sheath here.

GRIN. I knew it instantly; my suspicions were aroused —now they are confirmed: Kelmar is in league with these marauders; I found the door open,—you still slept. I searched the house for him; he is no where to be found, —he and his daughter have absconded. Now, sir, are you satisfied?

Count. I am. (*goes up stage*)

Karl. I am not; I wish we were safe at home. I'm no coward by day-light, but I hate adventures of this kind in the dark. Lord, how a man may be deceived! I took you for a great rogue; but I now find you are a good Christian enough, though you are a very ill-looking man.

Grin. Indeed; we can't all be as handsome as you are, you know.

Karl. (*pertly*) No, nor as witty as you are, you know.

Grin. Come, sir; follow me. (*going up to door,* R. C.) You can't mistake; see, 'tis day-break: at the cottage close to the narrow bridge that passes the ravine you will find repose.

Count. We'll follow you. *Exit* Grindoff, R. *door in flat.*

Karl. I don't half like that fellow yet. (*gets the portmanteau from* L. *table*) Now, the sooner we are off the better, sir. As for this fellow, the rats may take care of him. (Claudine *shrieks—heard without,* R. *door in flat*)

Count. (*drawing his sword*) Ha! a woman's voice! Karl, follow me!

Karl. What, more adventures! (*drawing his sword*) I'm ready. I say, (*to the body of* Riber) take care of the portmanteau, will you? *Exit* R. *door in flat, closed in.*

Scene Second.—*The Forest* (1st grooves)—*Stage partly dark.*

Music.—Enter Grindoff, *with* Claudine *in his arms.*

Count. (*without* R.) Karl! Karl! follow, this way!

Grin. (*resting,* C.) Ha, so closely pursued!—Nay, then——

    Going hastily, L., *he pushes aside the leaves of the secret pass, and they disappear,* L.

Enter Count Frederick Friberg, *hastily,* R.

Count. Gone! vanished! Can it be possible? Sure, 'tis witchcraft. I was close upon him—Karl! The cries of her he dragged with him, too, have ceased, and not the faintest echo of his retiring footsteps can be heard —Karl!

Enter KARL, R.

KARL. Oh, Lord! Pho! that hill's a breather! Why, where is he? Didn't you overtake him?

COUNT. No! in this spot he disappeared, and sunk, as it should seem, ghost like, into the very earth—Follow!

KARL. Follow!—Follow a will-o'-the-wisp!

COUNT. Quick—aid me to search!

KARL. Search out a ghost! Mercy on us! I'll follow you through the world, fight for you the best cock-giant robber of 'em all, but, if you're for hunting goblins, I'm off. Hey! where the devil's the woman, though? If she was a spirit, she made more noise than any lady alive.

COUNT. (L.) Perchance, the villain, so closely pursued, has destroyed his victim.

KARL. (R.) No doubt on't; he's killed her, to a certainty; nothing but death can stop a woman's tongue.

COUNT. (*having searched in vain*) From the miller we may gain assistance: Grindoff, no doubt, is acquainted with every turn and outlet of the forest; quick, attend me to the mill.   *Exeunt,* L.

KARL. Rat me if I'll run after the girl; why should I? girls never run after me. I know the tricks on 'em; they are all deceptions and full of mischief, like a barrel of gunpowder; they are like—they are like a lawsuit, and a lawsuit's like a devil's kettle, in which everything that's disagreeable is all boiled up together. None on 'em ever took delight in me, except it was to vex and jilt me. Ever since Wilhelmina slighted my passion, I have forsworn the sex, and all alone by myself have struggled through life, like a fly in treacle.   *Exit* KARL, R.

SCENE THIRD.—*The Cavern.*

Music.—ROBBERS *discovered asleep in different parts,* (R. *and* L.)—LOTHAIR *on guard, with a carbine, stands beneath the magazine—stage partly light.*

LOTH. (C.) Ere this it must be daylight—yet Grindoff

returns not—perchance their foul intent has failed—the fatal blow designed for Friberg may have fallen upon himself. How tedious drags the time, when fear, suspense, and doubt thus weigh upon the heart. Oh, Kelmar, beloved Claudine, you little know my peril. (*looks at the various groups of* BANDITTI, *and carefully rests his carbine at the foot of the rugged steps,* L. C., *leading to the magazine—he advances,* C.) While yet this drunken stupor makes their sleep most death-like, let me secure a terrible, but just revenge. If their infernal purpose be accomplished, this is their reward. (*draws a coil of fuse from his bosom*) These caverns, that spread beneath the mill, have various outlets, and in the fissures of the rock the train will lie unnoticed. Could I but reach the magazine.

Music—LOTHAIR *retires cautiously up,* C.—*he places his foot over the body of a* ROBBER, *who is seen asleep on the steps leading to the magazine—by accident he touches the carbine, which slips down—the* ROBBER, *being disturbed, alters his position, while* LOTHAIR *stands over him, and again reposes—*LOTHAIR *advances up the steps—as he arrives at the magazine,* WOLF'S *signal, the bugle, is heard from above—the* ROBBERS *instantly start up, and* LOTHAIR, *at the same moment, springs from the steps, and, seizing his carbine, stands in his previous attitude.*

Enter WOLF (GRINDOFF), *descending the steps of the opening,* L., *with* CLAUDINE *senseless in his arms.*

ROBBERS. The signal!

GOL. Wolf, we rejoice with you.

LOTH. (*advancing,* L.) Have you been successful?

WOLF. (*setting down* CLAUDINE) So far, at least, I have.

LOTH. (*aside*) Claudine—merciful powers! (*to* WOLF) But Kelmar——

WOLF. Shall not long escape me—Kelmar once secure, his favourite, my redoubted rival, young Lothair, may next require attention—bear her in, Golotz. (GOLOTZ *bears* CLAUDINE *off,* R. 1 E.) Where is Ravina?

Enter RAVINA, R. 2 E.

Oh, you are come!

RAVINA. I am; what is your will?

WOLF. That you attend Claudine; treat her as you would treat me.

RAVINA. I will, be sure on't.

WOLF. Look you, fail not. I cannot wait her recovery. —danger surrounds us.

ROBBERS. (*advancing*) Danger!

WOLF. Ay, every one must be vigilant, every heart resolved—Riber has been stabbed.

LOTH. Then Friberg——

WOLF. Has escaped.

LOTH. Thank heaven!

WOLF. How?

LOTH. Friberg is still reserved for me.

WOLF. Be it so—your firmness shall be proved.

RAVINA. So—one act of villany is spared you; pursue your fate no farther—desist, be warned in time.

WOLF. Fool! could woman's weakness urge me to retreat, my duty to our band would now make such repentance treachery.

ROBBERS. Noble captain!

WOLF. Mark you, my comrades: Kelmar has fled; left his house—no doubt for the Chateau Friberg. The suspicions of the Count are upon *him*. All mistrust of me is banished from his mind, and I have lured him and his companion to the cottage of our lost comrade, Riber.

LOTH. How came Claudine to fall into your power?

WOLF. I encountered her alone, as I left Kelmar's cottage. She had been to seek her father; I seized the opportunity, and conveyed her to the secret pass in the forest; her cries caused me to be pursued, and one instant later I had fallen into their hands—by this time they have recovered the path-way to the mill. Spiller shall supply Riber's place—be prepared to meet them at the Flask, and prove yourself——

LOTH. The man I am; I swear it.

WOLF. Enough—I am content!

RAVINA. (R.) Content! such guilt as thine can never feel content. Never will thy corroded heart have rest—years of security have made you rash, incautious—wanton in thy cruelty—and you will never rest until your mistaken policy destroys your band.

WOLF. No more of this—her discontent is dangerous. —Spiller! when you are prepared to leave the cavern, make fast the door; Ravina shall remain here confined until our work above is finished. (*aside to him*)

LOTH. I understand——

WOLF. Golotz and the rest—who are wont to cheer our revels with your music, be in waiting at the Flask, as travellers, wandering Savoyards, till the Count and his followers are safe within our toils; the delusion may spare us trouble. I know them resolute and fierce; and, should they once suspect, though our numbers overpower them, the purchase may cost us dear. Away—time presses—Spiller—remember——

LOTH. Fear me not—you soon shall know me.

Exit WOLF *and* ROBBERS *up the steps*, L. *in flat*—LO-THAIR *immediately runs up the steps to the maga-zine, and places the fuse within, closes the door and directs it towards the trap by which he first entered the cave*, R. U. E.

RAVINA. Now, then, hold firm, my heart and hand; one act of vengeance, one dreadful triumph, and I meet henceforth the hatred, the contempt of Wolf, without a sigh.

(*in great agitation—she advances to the table*, R. U. E., *and taking a vial from her bosom, pours the con-tents into a cup, and goes cautiously across to where* CLAUDINE *has been conducted.*

RAVINA. As she revives—ere yet her bewildered senses proclaim her situation, she will drink—and——

(LOTHAIR, *who has watched the conduct of* RAVINA, *seizes her arm, takes away the cup, and throws it off*, L.)

LOTH. Hold, mistaken woman! is this your pity for the unfortunate—of your own sex, too?—Are you the advocate of justice and of mercy—who dare condemn the cruelty of Wolf, yet with your own hand would destroy an innocent fellow-creature, broken-hearted, helpless, and forlorn?—Oh, shame! shame!

RAVINA.(R. C.) And who is he that dares to school me thus?

LOTH. Who am I?

RAVINA. Ay! that talk of justice and of mercy, yet pant to shed the blood of Friberg!

LOTH. (aside) Now, dared I trust her—I must, there is no resource, for they'll be left together. (to RAVINA) Ravina—say, what motive urged you to attempt an act that I must believe is hateful to your nature?

RAVINA. Have I not cause—ample cause?

LOTH. I may remove it.

RAVINA. Can you remove the pangs of jealousy?

LOTH. I can—Claudine will never be the bride of Wolf.

RAVINA. Who can prevent it?

LOTH. Her husband.

RAVINA. Is it possible?

LOTH. Be convinced. Claudine, Claudine! (Music)

CLAUD. (without, R.) Ha! that voice!

LOTH. (L. C.) Claudine!

CLAUD. (entering, R.) 'Tis he! 'tis he! then I am safe! Ah! who are these, and in what dreadful place am I?

LOTH. Beloved Claudine, can this disguise conceal me?

CLAUD. (R.) Lothair! I was not deceived.

(falls into his arms)

RAVINA. (L.) Lothair!

LOTH. (c.) Ay, her affianced husband. Ravina, our lives are in your power; preserve them and save yourself; one act of glorious repentance, and the blessings of the surrounding country are yours. Observe!

(Music—LOTHAIR points to the magazine—shows the train to RAVINA, and explains the intention—then gives a phosphorous bottle, which he shows the purpose of—she comprehends him—CLAUDINE'S action, expresses astonishment and terror—LOTHAIR opens the trap up the stage, R.)

RAVINA. Enough, I understand.

LOTH. (advancing) Be careful, be cautious, I implore you;—convey the train where I may distinctly see you from without the mill; and, above all, let no anxiety of mind, no fear of failure, urge you to fire the train till I give the signal. Remember, Claudine might be the victim of such fatal indiscretion.

RAVINA. But, Wolf. ——

Re-enter WOLF, *who hearing his name, halts at the back of the cavern.*

LOTH. Wolf, with his guilty companions, shall fall despised and execrated. (*seeing* WOLF) Ah! (*aside to* CLAUDINE) Remove the train.

WOLF. Villain! (C.. *levels a pistol at* LOTHAIR, R.—RAVINA *utters an exclamation of horror—* CLAUDINE *retreats, and removes the train to the foot of the steps*)

LOTH. (*retreating into* R. *corner*) Hold!—you are deceived.

WOLF. Do you acknowledge it?—But 'tis the last time. (*seizing* LOTHAIR *by the collar*)

LOTH. One moment.-

WOLF. What further deception?

LOTH. I have used none—hear the facts.

WOLF. What are they?

LOTH. Hatred to thee—jealousy of the fair Claudine, urged this woman to attempt her life. (*points to* CLAUDINE)

WOLF. Indeed!—for what purpose was that pass disclosed? (*pointing to the trap,* R.)

LOTH. I dared not leave them together.

WOLF. Vain subterfuge—your threat of destruction on me and my companions——

LOTH. Was a mere trick, a forgery, a fabrication to appease her disappointed spirit—induce her to quit the cave, and leave Claudine in safety.

WOLF. (*going up to, and closely observing* RAVINA) Plausible hypocrite, Ravina has no weapon of destruction —how then? (*crossing back to* LOTHAIR)

LOTH. (*looking towards* RAVINA, *who holds up the vial, unseen by* GRINDOFF) Ah! (*aside*) We are saved. (*crossing and snatching the vial, which she had retained in her hand*) Behold, let conviction satisfy your utmost doubts.

WOLF. (*looking on the label*) Poison!—you then are honest, Wolf unjust—I can doubt no longer. (*seizes* RAVINA *by the arm*) Fiend! descend instantly, in darkness and despair anticipate a dreadful punishment.

(*Music—* RAVINA *clasps her hands in entreaty, and descends the trap, which is closed violently by* WOLF)

WOLF. Now, Spiller, follow me to the Flask.   (*Music*)
Be sure, make fast yon upper door.

*(he takes his broad miller's hat, for which he had
returned—exit up steps,* L. *in flat,* LOTHAIR *following, and looking back significantly at* CLAUDINE,
*who then advances cautiously, opens the trap, and
gives the train to* RAVINA—*appropriate Music—*
RAVINA *and* CLAUDINE *remain in attitude, the latter
watching* LOTHAIR, *with uplifted hands)*

SCENE FOURTH.—*The Cottage of Riber—The sign of
"The Flask" at the door,* L. *in flat.*

Enter COUNT FREDERICK FRIBERG *and* KARL, R.

COUNT. This must be the house!

KARL. (R.) Clear as day-light; look, sir, "The Flask!"
Oh, and there stands the mill! (L.) I suppose old rough-and-
tough, master Grindoff, will be here presently. Well,
I'm glad we are in the right road at last; for such ins
and outs, and ups and downs, and circumbendibuses in
that forest, I never——

COUNT. (L.) True; we may now obtain guides and
assistance to pursue that ruffian!

KARL. (*aside*) Pursue again!—not to save all the she
sex!—flesh and blood can't stand this.

COUNT. (*abstracted*) Yet, after so long an absence,
delay is doubly irksome—could I but see her my heart
doats on!

KARL. Ab! could *I* but see what my heart doats on.

COUNT. M, sweet Laurette!

KARL. A dish of saur-kraut!

COUNT. (*crosses to* R.) Fool!

KARL. Fool! so I mustn't enjoy a good dinner even
in imagination.

COUNT. Still complaining!

KARL. How can I help it, sir? I can't live upon air,
as you do.

COUNT. You had plenty last night.

KARL. So I had last Christmas, sir; and what sort of
a supper was it, after all?—One apple, two pears, three
bunches of sour grapes, and a bowl of milk: one of your

D

forest meals—I can't abide such a cruel cold diet—oh, for a bumper of brandy! but, unfortunately, my digestion keeps pace with my appetite—I'm always hungry. Oh, for a bumper of brandy!

(*Music heard within the " Flask," L. in flat.*)

COUNT. Hush!

KARL. What's that? Somebody tickling a guitar into fits; soft music always makes me doleful.

COUNT. Go into the house—stay; remember, I would be private.

KARL. Private—in a public-house. Oh, I understand, incog. But the miller knows you, sir.

COUNT. That's no reason all his people should.

KARL. I smoke—they'd be awed by our dignity and importance—poor things, I pity 'em—they are not used to polished society. Holloa! house! landlord! Mr. Flask.

Enter LOTHAIR, L. *door in flat, as landlord.*

KARL. Good entertainment here for man and beast, I'm told.

LOTH. You are right.

KARL. Well, here am I, and there's my master!

LOTH. You are welcome. (*aside*) I dare not say otherwise; Wolf is on the watch.

(GRINDOFF *appears, watching at a window*, L. *in flat*)

KARL. Have you got anything ready? (*smacking his lips*)

LOTH. Too much, I fear.

KARL. Not a bit, I'll warrant. I'm devilish sharp set.

LOTH. Well, you are just in time.

KARL. Pudding-time, I hope! have you got any meat?

LOTH. I must ask him. (*aside and looking round anxiously*) Won't your master——

KARL. No! he lives upon love; but don't be alarmed, —I'll make it worth your while; I'm six meals in arrear, and can swallow enough for both of us.

Exit KARL, *with* LOTHAIR, *to the " Flask,"* L. *door in flat—*GRINDOFF *closes the window.*

COUNT. Yes, I'm resolved—the necessity for passing the river must by this time have urged the peasantry to re-establish the ferry—delay is needless. I'll away instantly to the Chateau Friberg, and with my own people return to redress the wrongs of my oppressed and suffering tenantry.

Enter KARL, L. door in flat.

COUNT. Well, your news?

KARL. Glorious!—The landlord, Mr. Flask, is a man after my own heart, a fellow of five meals a day.

COUNT. Psha! who are the musicians?

KARL. Ill-looking dogs, truly;—Savoyards, I take it; one plays on a thing like a frying-pan, the other turns something that sounds like a young grindstone.

COUNT. What else?

KARL. As fine an imitation of a shoulder of mutton as ever I clapp'd my eyes on.

Enter KELMAR, exhausted by haste and fatigue, R.

COUNT. Kelmar!

KELM. Ah, the Count and his companion!—Thank heaven, I am arrived in time! my master will be saved, though Claudine, my poor unhappy child, is lost. Fly, I beseech you, fly from this spot! Do not question me; this is no time for explanations; one moment longer, and you are betrayed—your lives irrecoverably sacrificed.

COUNT. Would you again deceive us?

KELM. I have been myself deceived—fatally deceived! let an old man's prayers prevail with you! Leave, oh leave this accursed place, and——

Enter WOLF, in his miller's dress, L. door in flat, he advances, C.

KELM. Ah, the miller! then has hope forsaken me—Yet one ray, one effort more, and——

WOLF. (C.) Thy treachery is known. (*he seizes KELMAR by the collar*)

KELM. (R.) One successful effort more, and death is welcome.

WOLF. Villain!

KELM. Thou art the villain—see—behold!

(*with a violent effort of strength, the old man suddenly turns upon* GRINDOFF, *and tears open his vest, beneath which he appears armed—*WOLF, *at the same instant, dashes* KELMAR *from him, who, impelled to* R., *is caught by the* COUNT—*the* COUNT *draws his sword—*WOLF, L., *draws pistols in each hand from his belt, and his hat falls off at the same instant— tableau—appropriate Music*)

COUNT. 'Tis he! the same! 'tis Wolf.

WOLF. Spiller! Golotz!   *Rushes out*, L.

KARL. Is it Wolf? Damn his pistols! This shall reach him. (*draws his sword, and hastens after* WOLF, L. *—the report of a pistol is immediately heard*, L.

Exit COUNT FRIBERG *and* KELMAR, L.—*At the same moment*, GOLOTZ *and another* ROBBER, *disguised as minstrels, followed by* LOTHAIR, *burst from the house*, L. *door in flat.*

GOLOT. (L.) We are called; Wolf called us!—Ah, they have discovered him!

LOTH. 'Tis too late to follow him, he has reached the bridge.

GOLOT. Then he is safe; but see, at the foot of the hill, armed men, in the Friberg uniform, press forward to the mill.

LOTH. This way we must meet them, then; in, to the subterranean pass! *Exeunt* GOLOTZ *and* ROBBER, *to house.*

LOTH. Now, Claudine, thy sufferings shall cease, and thy father's wrongs shall be revenged.   *Exit, to house.*

SCENE FIFTH.—*A near View of the Mill*, C., *standing on an elevated projection—from the stage a narrow bridge, to rise and fall, passes to the rock*, R. C., *on the platform of which stands the mill.*

Music—Enter RAVINA, L. U. E., *ascending the ravine with the fuse, which she places carefully in the crannies of the rock*, L.

RAVINA. My toil is over; the train is safe. From this spot I may receive the signal from Lothair, and, at one blow, the hapless victims of captivity and insult are amply, dreadfully avenged. (*Music—a pistol is fired without,* L. 2 E.) Ah, Wolf!   *She retires,* L. U. E.

Enter WOLF, L., *as pursued, and turning, fires his remaining pistol off,* L., *then hurries across the bridge, which he instantly draws up*—KARL *rushes on,* L.

WOLF. (*with a shout of great exultation*) Ha, ha! you strive in vain!

KARL. Cowardly rascal! you'll be caught at last.
    (*shaking his sword at* WOLF)

WOLF. By whom?

KARL. Your only friend, Beelzebub: run as fast as you will, he'll trip up your heels at last.

WOLF. Fool-hardy slave, I have sworn never to descend from this spot alive, unless with liberty.

KARL. Oh, we'll accommodate you; you shall have *liberty* to *ascend* from it; the wings of your own mill shall be the gallows, and fly with every rascal of you into the other world.

WOLF. Golotz!—Golotz, I say! (*calling towards the mill*)

Enter COUNT FRIBERG, *with* KELMAR *and the* ATTENDANTS *from the Chateau Friberg, in uniform, and armed,* L., *they cross to* R.

COUNT. Wretch! your escape is now impossible. Surrender to the injured laws of your country.

WOLF. Never! the brave band that now await my commands within the mill double your number. Golotz!

Enter GOLOTZ *from a small door in the mill,* C.

WOLF. Quick! let my bride appear.
    Exit GOLOTZ, C. *door in flat.*

Enter RAVINA, L. 2 E.—WOLF *starts.*

RAVINA. She is here! What would you?

WOLF. Ravina!—Traitress!

RAVINA. Traitress! What, then, art thou? But I come not here to parley; ere it be too late, make one atonement for thy injuries—restore this old man's child.

KELM. Does she still live?

WOLF. She does; but not for thee, or for the youth Lothair.

RAVINA. Obdurate man! then do I know my course.

Re-enter LOTHAIR, *conducting* CLAUDINE *from the mill, a cloak concealing him.*

CLAUD. Oh, my dear father!

KELM. (R.) My child—Claudine! Oh, spare, in pity spare her!

WOLF. Now mark me, Count: unless you instantly withdraw your followers, and let my troop pass free, by my hand she dies!

KELM. Oh, mercy!

COUNT. Hold yet a moment!

WOLF. Withdraw your followers.

COUNT. Till thou art yielded up to justice, they never shall depart.

WOLF. For that threat, be this your recompense!

LOTH. (*throwing aside his cloak*) And this my triumph.

(*Music*—LOTHAIR *places himself before* CLAUDINE, *and receives* WOLF'S *attack—the* ROBBER *is wounded, staggers back, sounds his bugle, and the mill is crowded with* BANDITTI—LOTHAIR *throws back the bridge, catches* CLAUDINE *in his arms, upon his release from* WOLF, *and hurries upon the bridge*)

LOTH. (*crossing the bridge with* CLAUDINE *in his arms*) Ravina, fire the train.

(RAVINA *instantly sets fire to the fuse, the flash of which is seen to run down the side of the rock into the gully under the bridge, and the explosion immediately takes place*—KELMAR, *rushing forward, catches* CLAUDINE *in his arms*)

www.ingramcontent.com/pod-product-compliance
Lightning Source LLC
Chambersburg PA
CBHW081305040426
42452CB00014B/2654